QUIZ QUEST

QUIZ AND ACTIVITY BOOK

Published by Ladybird Books Ltd 2012
A Penguin Company
Penguin Books Ltd, 80 Strand, London, WC2R 0RL, UK
Penguin Group (USA) Inc., 375 Hudson Street, New York 10014, USA
Penguin Books Australia Ltd, 707 Collins Street, Melbourne, Victoria 3008, Australia
Australia (A division of Pearson Australia Group Pty Ltd)
Canada, India, New Zealand, South Africa

Written by Cavan Scott
Sunbird is a trademark of Ladybird Books Ltd

www.ladybird.com

ISBN: 978-1-40939-170-8
001
Printed in Great Britain

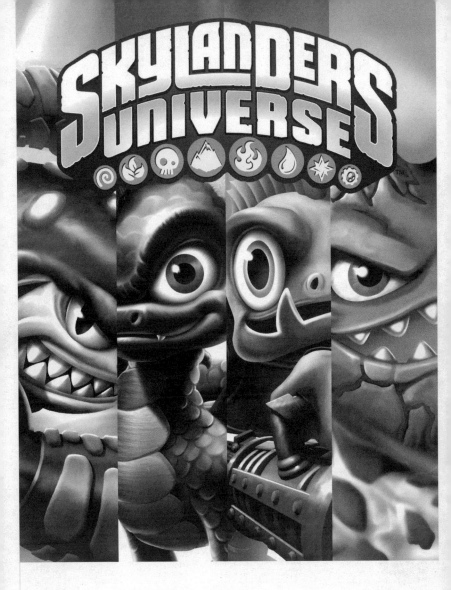

QUIZ QUEST

QUIZ AND ACTIVITY BOOK

CONTENTS

Prepare Yourself!	8
Skylands Secrets	10
Friends and Allies	13
The Magic Element	16
Spyro	19
Word Warriors	
Crossword	22
Hidden Word	24
Double Puzzle	25
The Water Element	27
Gill Grunt	30
Pirate Attack!	33
Battle Cry Bonanza	36
Logic Puzzles	
Eon's Hat Hunt	40
Going for Gold	42
Meal Muddle	44
The Fire Element	48
Eruptor	51
Power Mixup	54

The Air Element 57

Lightning Rod 60

What's the Question? 63

Word Warriors
  Skylander Search 66
  Kriss Kross 68

The Life Element 71

Stump Smash 74

Weapons at the Ready 77

Word Warriors
  Pathfinder 80
  Match Blocks 82
  Riddle-me-ree 84

Kaos' Mind-melting Quizzes
of DOOM! 86
  Ultimate Kaos 88
  Memory Buster 91
  Trolls on Parade 92
  Cyclops 94
  Countdown 97
  Evil Wordsearch 98
  Beware the Minions of Kaos 102

The Undead Element 106

Hex 109

Anagramania! 112

Picture Puzzles
Count the Symbols 115
Odd One Out 116
Shadow Dragon 118
Slice 'n' Dice 120

The Earth Element 122

Terrafin 125

Who's Who? 128

Armed and Dangerous 132

The Tech Element 135

Trigger Happy 138

The Arkeyans 141

Word Warriors
Search for the Elements 144
Spiral 146
Crazy Crossout 148
Secret Friend 150

Odd Ones Out 154

That's not my Upgrade   157

Personality Test   160

Undead Funny   164

Blitzed Battle Cries   166

Word Warriors
    Word Count   170
    Code Breaker   172

Which Skylander Are You?   174

Master Eon's Mega Quiz   180

Final Score   190

PREPARE YOURSELF!

Welcome, young Portal Master. The time has come to embark upon an incredible quest. Do you know the difference between a chompie and a cyclops? Is your ancient Skylands history up to scratch? Can you remember which Skylander was tricked into donning cursed armour or who saw off a band of dragon hunters single-handedly?

Above all, how well do you know our enemies?

Turn the page to embark upon your journey, keeping a note of your score as you go. Overcome the hurdles ahead and you may just prove yourself ready to take your place among the Portal Master elite.

Good luck.

Master Eon

SKYLANDS SECRETS

How good is your Skylands knowledge?

1 **How many floating islands make up Skylands?**

- **A** 1,000
- **B** 10,000
- **C** No one knows – there are too many to count

2 **Why is Skylands so important?**

- **A** From here you can travel anywhere in the universe
- **B** It's where the first sheep was born
- **C** It's a wonderful family holiday destination

3 Portal Masters use Portals of Power to travel from island to island, but can they also be used to travel in time?

A Yes
B No

4 Which race of legendary beings built the Core of Light?

A The Arkeyans
B The Benevolent Ancients
C The Elder Elementals

5 What is the name of the race of furry folk that are found all across Skylands?

A Mabu
B Manu
C Malu

6 What is the main function of the Core of Light?

A To keep the Darkness at bay
B To remind Master Eon where he lives
C To provide Skylanders with their powers

7 Which of the following is <u>not</u> one of the eight Elements that make up the Core of Light?

A Earth
B Mind
C Tech

8 True or False: the first Skylanders were called The Monoliths.

A True

B False

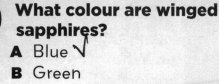

9 What colour are winged sapphires?

A Blue

B Green

C Red

10 Throughout its history, courageous explorers and brave pioneers have searched for the edge of Skylands. Many have been lost in an unnatural force of nature – but what is its name?

A The Terrifying White Twirling Tornado

B The Great Black Whirl Storm

C The Awesome Scarlet Rolling Whirlwind

MY SCORE

/10

FRIENDS AND ALLIES

All about the Skylanders' best buddies.

1 Eon wasn't always an all-powerful Portal Master. What was his original job?

A A pan polisher
B A shepherd boy ✓
C A strawberry picker

2 What was the name of Eon's mentor?

A Cattylumpo ✓
B Mattyhumpo
C Nattybumpo

3 What colour is the crystal on the end of Eon's staff?

A Blue
B Red ✓
C Yellow

4 Hugo is Eon's right hand Mabu and chief librarian, but what kind of animal is he scared of?

A Cows
B Pigs
C Sheep ✓

5 Hugo once told Cali a whopping great lie. What was it?

A He told her that he was the fastest Mabu in all of Skylands

B He told her he built the Core of Light

C He told her that he was Flynn's long lost brother

6 Hugo's hero (other than Master Eon of course) is Skylands' most famous historian. What is the scholar's name?

A Professor P. Grungally

B Professor E. Rootworthy

C Professor T. Brangully

7 What is Flynn's favourite mode of transport?

A Trains

B Planes

C Hot air balloons

8 In days gone by, Cali was one of Skylands' most adventurous explorers. How does she spend her time now?

A Growing vegetables

B Training Skylanders by setting Heroic Challenges

C Basket weaving

9 **What is Flynn's catchphrase?**
   A Zoom!
   B Foom!
   C Boom!

10 **What kind of creature is Persephone?**
   A A fairy
   B A goblin
   C A giant

THE MAGIC ELEMENT

Can you conjure up the answers to these questions?

1 The ancient Arkeyans discovered the glistening oil that flows through all things Magic (even sheep). What is its name?

A Quickserum

B Quicksilver

C Quick Drying Cement

2 Voodood belongs to a brave and magical tribe of orcs, known as . . .

A The Ooga Warriors

B The Booger Warriors

C The Super-Dooper Warriors

3 What is Wrecking Ball?

A A living cannonball

B A mutant blueberry

C A super-sized grub

4 Double Trouble wears a mask made of . . .
- **A** Wood
- **B** Concrete
- **C** Bone

5 What is the name of Voodood's legendary weapon?
- **A** The Axe Lever
- **B** The Axe Cleaver
- **C** The Axe Reaver

6 How did Wrecking Ball grow so big?
- **A** He was caught in one of Kaos' spells
- **B** He gobbled up a magic stew
- **C** He didn't. Everything else in Skylands shrank

7 When he was a young spellcaster, Double Trouble ate a rare flower called the Whispering Water Lily. What special power did the plant grant him?
- **A** The power of flight
- **B** The ability to turn invisible
- **C** The ability to create exploding clones

8 **Where did Voodood find his mighty axe?**
A The Cave of Trials
B The Cave of Terrors
C The Cave of Wonders

9 **Voodood's tribe was eventually destroyed by which evil force?**
A Occulous
B Malefor the Undead Dragon King
C The Darkness

What is the name of the energy that flows from Double Trouble's staff?
10 **A** Elven
B Eldritch
C Elvis

SPYRO

True or False – are you a Spyro super fan?

1 **Spyro was born in Skylands.**
TRUE ☐ FALSE ☐

2 **The Scrolls of the Ancients mention many of Spyro's past adventures.**
TRUE ☐ FALSE ☐

3 **Spyro cannot fly.**
TRUE ☐ FALSE ☐

4 When he jumps through a portal, Spyro yells his famous battlecry: "In A Flap!"

TRUE ☐   FALSE ☐

5 Spyro can harness more than just the Magic Element. He's strong in all the other Elements too.

TRUE ☐   FALSE ☐

6 Spyro freed Drobot from the thrall of the Undead Dragon King Malefor.

TRUE ☐   FALSE ☐

7 Spyro can absorb dark Magic and use it against the forces of evil. Oooh, creepy!

TRUE ☐   FALSE ☐

ANSWERS

1 False – He comes from a land far, far away. No, even further than that!

2 True – They couldn't get enough of him.

3 False – Although he can't fly that high!

4 False – He's more likely to yell "All Fired Up!"

5 True – He's the ultimate all-rounder.

6 False – It was Cynder he rescued.

7 True – The process worries his fellow Skylanders at times.

8 True – He's a good dragon to have around.

9 False – He turns a darker (and spookier) shade of purple!

10 False – It's a devastating dive-bomb head smash.

MY SCORE /10

8 Spyro's no dummy. He has an encyclopedic knowledge of every world that falls under his protection.

TRUE ☐ FALSE ☐

9 When channeling dark Magic, Spyro turns red.

TRUE ☐ FALSE ☐

10 Spyro's Earth Pound upgrade allows him to grow money trees. Cha-ching!

TRUE ☐ FALSE ☐

WORD WARRIORS

Crossword

Across

4 Skylands' finest balloonist (5)

5 An explosive-loving brute (5)

8 The ancient rulers of Skylands (8)

10 & 15 Skeletal archers:
_____ 'n' _____ (4, 6)

12 _____ of Power (6)

14 6 down's assistant (4)

Down

1 The Water _____ (7)

2 A creepy Element (6)

3 A small fire creature (5,3)

6 Clam-tron 4000 is one (5)

7 The Greatest Portal Master of them all (6,3)

9 ----- Smash (5)

11 Eruptor likes relaxing in pools of this (4)

13 A bamboo wanderer (4)

14 A Skylander of the Element found in
2 down (3)

MY
SCORE

/16

23

Hidden Word

Can you find the words hidden in these sentences? Here's one so you can see how it's done:

"This sheep wool pie has gone of**f I re**ckon," said Ghost Roaster.
The hidden word is **FIRE**.

CLUE
They're all
Elements!

1 Eon asked Hugo to note changes in the weather.

2 Drobot repaired his blade gears.

3 Terrafin burrowed below a termite hill.

4 Flynn's balloon started to appear through the mist.

5 Cali felt on top of the world.

MY SCORE /5

Double Puzzle

Unscramble each of the clue words to find a Skylander.

ILGL NGRUT

BRUNUSN

HASB

POSRY

EBORMO

OKOZ

NADROAW

RTOP RUE

For an extra point, take the letters that appear in shaded boxes and unscramble them to find something scary.

Crossword

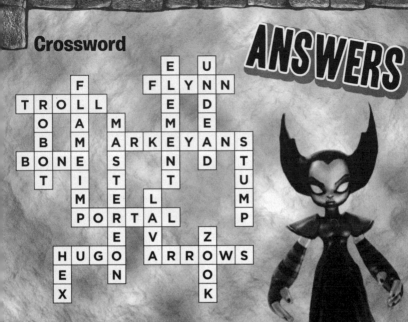

Crossword grid:

```
                E   U
        F     F L Y N N
T R O L L     L   E
O     A   M   E   N
B     M   A R K E Y A N S
B O N E   S   E   D   T
T     I   T   N       U
      M   E   T       M
      P O R T A L     P
          E   L   Z
    H U G O   A R R O W S
    H E     N     O
    E X           O
    X             K
```

Double Puzzle

```
G I L L   G R U N T
S U N B U R N
B A S H
S P Y R O
B O O M E R
Z O O K
W A R N A D O
E R U P T O R
```

The shaded boxes spell **THE DARKNESS**

Hidden words

1 Eon asked Hugo to no**TE CH**anges in the weather.

2 Drobot rep**AIR**ed his blade gears.

3 Terrafin burrowed belo**W A TER**mite hill.

4 Flynn's balloon started to app**EAR TH**rough the mist.

5 Ca**LI FE**lt on top of the world.

THE WATER ELEMENT

True or False – dive into these aquatic quandaries.

1 **Slam Bam is an ice ogre.**
TRUE ☐   FALSE ☐

2 **Kaos destroyed Slam Bam's floating iceberg just because the Skylander made better sandwiches than him.**
TRUE ☐   FALSE ☐

3 **Slam Bam has six frosty arms.**
TRUE ☐   FALSE ☐

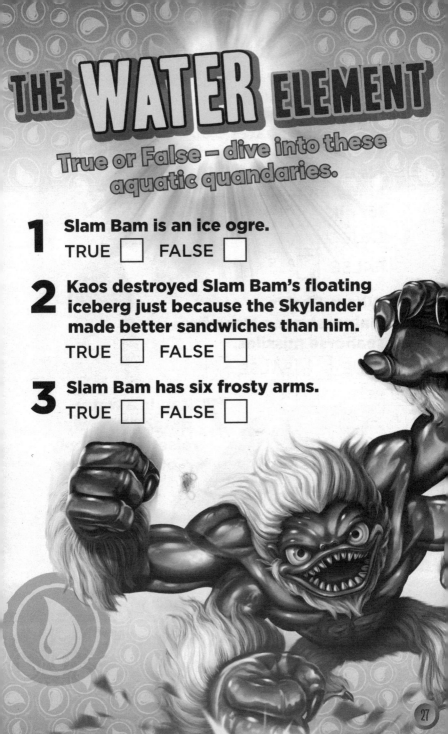

4 Wham-Shell, the crusading crustacean, is a royal prince.

TRUE ☐ FALSE ☐

5 Wham-Shell hates trolls because they invaded his underwater kingdom to drill for oil.

TRUE ☐

FALSE ☐

6 Wham-Shell's Malacostracan Mace fires seahorse missiles.

TRUE ☐ FALSE ☐

7 Zap is a water dragon who was raised by a family of electric eels.

TRUE ☐

FALSE ☐

MY
SCORE
/10

8 Zap was given a special electrified golden crown that is always fully charged to give bad guys a shock!

TRUE ☐

FALSE ☐

9 Zap can slide into battle on slippery sea slime.

TRUE ☐ FALSE ☐

10 The two-legged sea creatures that live on beaches and will try to cut off your ankles with their sawlike bills are called saw ducks.

TRUE ☐ FALSE ☐

GILL GRUNT

It's time for Gill Power!

1 **Gill Grunt is a . . .**
- **A** Fishman
- **B** Gillman
- **C** Finman

2 **Which of the following isn't one of Gill's battle cries?**
- **A** Fins of Fury!
- **B** Follow the Freak!
- **C** Fear the Fish!

3 When he was younger, Gill fell head over fins in love with a beautiful girl. Ahhhhh. But what kind of girl was she?

A A sharkwoman
B A squidlass
C A mermaid

4 Where did Gill meet his girlfriend?

A A misty lagoon
B A smelly swamp
C A choppy lake

5 Which of the following is one of Gill's power upgrades?

A Whirlpool Cannon
B Anchor Cannon
C Octopus Cannon

6 Who kidnapped Gill's girlfriend?

A Kaos
B Trolls
C Pirates

7 Gill was sent by Master Eon to ask which watery warrior to become a Skylander?

A Wham-Shell
B Slam Bam
C Zap

8 Which of these upgrades allows Gill to fly?

A Fishy Flight
B Thruster Flight
C Booster Flight

9 How many prongs do Gill's Quadent Harpoons have?

A Two
B Three
C Four

10 What happens to the starfish that Gill fires out of his Neptune Gun?

A They explode
B They grow to huge proportions
C They eat anything in their path

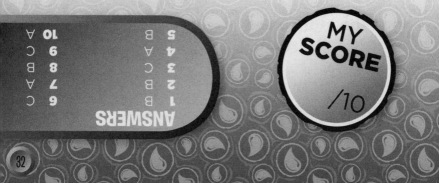

MY SCORE

/10

PIRATE ATTACK!

Ten teasers about the terrors of the sea

1 **What is the name of the scurviest and most villainous of all pirate captains?**
- **A** Captain Dreaddog
- **B** Captain Dreadbeard
- **C** Captain Dreadbrow

2 **What kind of creature is the Captain?**
- **A** Gillman
- **B** Squiddler
- **C** Seadog

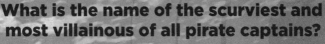

3 **How many eyes does the Captain hide under eyepatches?**
- **A** None **B** One **C** Six

4 What game does the Captain love playing?
   A Pirate cards
   B Pirate football
   C Pirate memory game

5 What is the name of the Captain's special deck of cards?
   A Anchor deck
   B Skull deck
   C Mermaid deck

6 What fires out of a squiddler's gun?
   A Catfish   B Starfish   C Blowfish

7 What colour is the skin of the squidface brutes?
   A Orange
   B Blue
   C Pink

8 What weapons do the squidface brutes wield?
   A Anchors
   B Axes
   C Swords

9 What other type of pirate uses the same kind of weapon as the squidface brutes?

A Seadog skippers

B Captain K9s

C Sky pirates

10 What do seadog pirates use to attack Skylanders?

A Guns

B Sea cucumbers

C Cutlasses

MY SCORE /10

ANSWERS

1 B
2 C
3 B
4 A
5 B
6 C
7 CB
8 A
9 B
10 C

BATTLE CRY BONANZA

Can you match the battle cry to the Skylander?

1 **Twists of Fury!**
- **A** Warnado
- **B** Whirlwind
- **C** Sonic Boom

TWISTS OF FURY!

BLINK AND DESTROY!

2 **Blink and Destroy!**
- **A** Drobot
- **B** Drill Sergeant
- **C** Boomer

3 **Armed and Dangerous!**
- **A** Slam Bam
- **B** Stump Smash
- **C** Terrafin

ARMED AND DANGEROUS!

FEAR THE DARK!

4 Fear the Dark!
A Ghost Roaster
B Cynder
C Hex

5 Rock and Roll!
A Prism Break
B Bash
C Dino-Rang

ROCK AND ROLL!

SLASH AND BURN!

6 Slash and Burn!
A Eruptor
B Flameslinger
C Ignitor

FRUIT PUNCH!

7 Fruit Punch!
- **A** Camo
- **B** Zook
- **C** Stealth Elf

BOOM SHOCK-A-LAKA!

8 Boom Shock-A-Laka!
- **A** Boomer
- **B** Trigger Happy
- **C** Double Trouble

SLICE AND DICE!

9 Slice and Dice!
- **A** Voodood
- **B** Chop Chop
- **C** Sunburn

ONE STRIKE AND YOU'RE OUT! **10**

One Strike and You're Out!
- **A** Lightning Rod
- **B** Zap
- **C** Spyro

11 **Roast 'n' Toast!**
- **A** Ignitor
- **B** Sunburn
- **C** Flameslinger

ROAST 'N' TOAST!

NO CHAIN, NO GAIN!

12 **No Chain, No Gain!**
- **A** Wham-Shell
- **B** Voodood
- **C** Ghost Roaster

MY SCORE

/12

ANSWERS

C	12	C	6
B	11	B	5
B	10	A	4
C	9	C	3
C	8	A	2
A	7	B	1

LOGIC PUZZLES

Eon's Hat Hunt

I have sent three of my Skylanders off to find the locations of three special hats. From the clues below, work out which Skylander found which hat and where! If you work it all out correctly, give yourself **six whole points** from me.

CLUES

1   The Skylander who searched the Core of Light did not find the Birthday Hat.

2   Trigger Happy, who found the Spiked Hat, did not search underground.

3   Spyro, who did not search the Core of Light, found a hat belonging to a military man.

4   Gill Grunt did not search the Cloud Kingdom.

	HATS			PLACES		
	Birthday Hat	General's Hat	Spiked Hat	The Core of Light	The Cloud Kingdom	Arkeyan Mines
SKYLANDERS Gill Grunt						
Trigger Happy						
Spyro						
PLACES The Core of Light						
The Cloud Kingdom						
Arkeyan Mines						

MY SCORE

/6

Going for Gold

Three Skylanders have taken part in the Skylands Sports Day. Can you work out which sport they played and what medal they received? Give yourself six points if you work it out correctly!

CLUES

1 The Skylander who won the gold medal was not a dragon.

2 Camo did not take part in the Sheep Tossing contest.

3 Whirlwind won a silver medal, but not in Toe Wrestling.

4 Lightning Rod took part in Mammoth Lifting.

	MEDALS			SPORTS		
	Gold	Silver	Bronze	Sheep Tossing	Toe Wrestling	Mammoth Lifting
SKYLANDERS Whirlwind						
Camo						
Lightning Rod						
SPORTS Sheep Tossing						
Toe Wrestling						
Mammoth Lifting						

MY
SCORE
/6

43

Meal Muddle

Looking at these clues, can you work out who ate what and for which meal? You get six points if you find the right answers.

CLUES

1 Hugo hates sheep wool pizza.

2 The person who had barbecued dragon wings had already eaten two meals that day.

3 Flynn ate sheep wool pizza, but not for lunch.

4 Kaos ate at supper time, but didn't have popping pretzels.

		FOOD			MEAL		
		Sheep wool pizza	Barbecued dragon wings	Popping pretzels	Breakfast	Lunch	Supper
CHARACTERS	Flynn						
	Kaos						
	Hugo						
MEAL	Breakfast						
	Lunch						
	Supper						

MY SCORE /6

Hat Hunt

	Birthday Hat	General's Hat	Spiked Hat	The Core of Light	The Cloud Kingdom	Arkeyan Mines
Gill Grunt	O	X	X	X	X	O
Trigger Happy	X	X	O	O	X	X
Spyro	X	O	X	X	O	X
The Core of Light	X	X	O			
The Cloud Kingdom	X	O	X			
Arkeyan Mines	O	X	X			

Going for Gold

	Gold	Silver	Bronze	Sheep Tossing	Toe Wrestling	Mammoth Lifting
Whirlwind	X	O	X	O	X	X
Camo	X	X	O	X	O	X
Lightning Rod	O	X	X	X	X	O
Sheep Tossing	X	O	X			
Toe Wrestling	X	X	O			
Mammoth Lifting	O	X	X			

Meal Muddle

	Sheep wool pizza	Barbecued dragon wings	Popping pretzels	Breakfast	Lunch	Supper
Flynn	O	X	X	O	X	X
Kaos	X	O	X	X	X	O
Hugo	X	X	O	X	O	X
Breakfast	O	X	X			
Lunch	X	X	O			
Supper	X	O	X			

THE FIRE ELEMENT

10 burning questions to answer

1 What kind of creature is Flameslinger?

A An elf
B A troll
C A fire spirit

2 When Flameslinger was just a child, he became world-famous. Why?

A He could fire flames out of his fingertips, toes and, er, elbows
B He could see visions of faraway places, looking through fires as if they were crystal balls
C His hair was red hot. You could even cook eggs on it

3 Sunburn is half dragon, half what?

A Fire imp   **B** Phoenix   **C** Wyvern

4 When he rescued a fire spirit from drowning in a pond, Flameslinger was rewarded with an enchanted bow and magical fire boots. What special power did the boots grant him?

A He would never have smelly socks ever again

B He could rocket into the sky on columns of fire

C He could run at blistering speeds

5 What colour is Flameslinger's stylish blindfold?

A Red

B Green

C Blue

6 Sunburn's flamethrower breath can fry the forces of Darkness to a crisp, but what other unique gift does he possess?

A He can teleport from place to place

B He can shoot fiery arrows from his eyes

C He can create burning doubles of himself

7 **Why is Sunburn often hunted by wicked sorcerers and bounty hunters?**

A They want to have him for roast dinner

B His claws can open any lock in Skylands

C They want to use his feathers in their diabolical potions and spells

8 **What is Sunburn's battle cry?**

A "Roast 'n' Toast!"

B "If you can't stand the heat!"

C "Rise and shine!"

9 **What was Ignitor's original name when he was a knight?**

A Infernio

B Ignatius

C Brian

10 **How did Ignitor get transformed into a flaming, sword-swinging fire spirit?**

A He was hit by one of Flameslinger's hellfire arrows

B While rescuing a fair maiden he fell into a bubbling enchanted volcano

C A witch tricked him into putting on a suit of cursed armour

MY SCORE

/10

50

ERUPTOR

True or False – show off your sizzling knowledge of the searing Skylander!

1 Eruptor was born on top of a volcano.

TRUE ☐   FALSE ☐

2 His home was destroyed during a fight at a lava pool party.

TRUE ☐   FALSE ☐

3 The people of Skylands have always known about Lava Beasts like Eruptor.

TRUE ☐   FALSE ☐

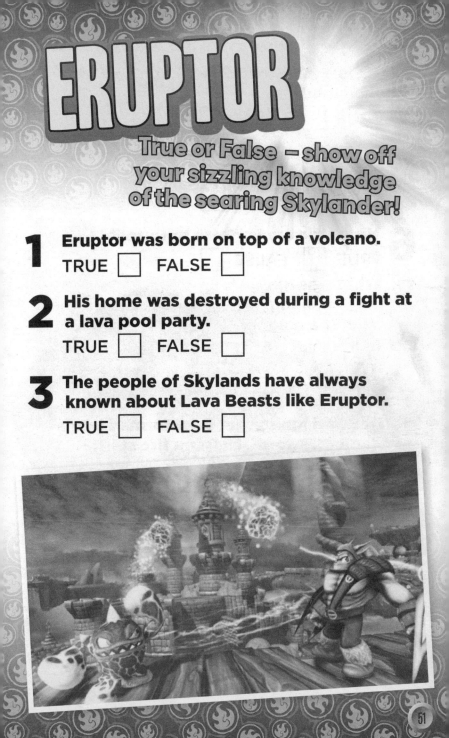

4 He is a mild-mannered, calm sort of Skylander.

TRUE ☐   FALSE ☐

5 Eruptor can lob balls of lava from his hands!

TRUE ☐   FALSE ☐

6 His battle cry is "Born to Burp!"

TRUE ☐   FALSE ☐

7 If he receives the right upgrade, Eruptor can cause fiery volcanos to form from the ground.

TRUE ☐ FALSE ☐

8 Eruptor loves being in crowds.

TRUE ☐ FALSE ☐

9 Lava kings, the nastiest lava beasts, belch out fire imps.

TRUE ☐ FALSE ☐

10 Eruptor's super upgrade is known as 'Mega Magma Balls'

TRUE ☐ FALSE ☐

MY SCORE /10

ANSWERS

1 False. He was born underneath a volcanic island.

2 True. The entire island was destroyed when tempers boiled over.

3 False. Their existence only became widely known when they were spewed out of their volcanic home.

4 False. He's always ready to blow his top.

5 True. Enemies beware!

6 False. It's "Born to Burn!"

7 True. It's called his 'Revenge of Prometheus' move.

8 False. Crowds make him seriously lose his cool.

9 True. They're lava-packed lackies of Kaos!

10 True. It produces a belch and a half!

POWER MIXUP

Persephone provides Skylanders with upgrades to their already awesome abilities. Can you match the upgrades with the right Skylanders?

1 Starfishicus Giganticus
- A Gill Grunt
- B Terrafin
- C Wham-Shell

2 Beast of Conflagration
- A Eruptor
- B Sunburn
- C Lightning Rod

3 Stonefist Traps
- A Prism Break
- B Dino-Rang
- C Drill Sergeant

4 Ibex's Wrath Charge
- A Spyro
- B Wrecking Ball
- C Cynder

5 **Pot O' Gold**
A Boomer
B Zook
C Trigger Happy

6 **Searing Sun Blast**
A Ignitor
B Camo
C Flameslinger

7 **Metalhead**
A Drobot
B Sonic Boom
C Ghost Roaster

8 **Dragon Flight**
- **A** Whirlwind
- **B** Dark Spyro
- **C** Bash

9 **Wall of Bones**
- **A** Hex
- **B** Chop Chop
- **C** Double Trouble

10 **Havoc Smash**
- **A** Stump Smash
- **B** Boomer
- **C** Voodood

ANSWERS

1 C	2 A	3 B
4 A	5 C	6 B
7 C	8 A	9 A
10 B		

MY SCORE

/10

THE AIR ELEMENT

True or False – ten breezy brain-busters

1 **Whirlwind is half-dragon, half-rhino.**
TRUE ☐   FALSE ☐

2 **Whirlwind can blast rainbow energy from her horn.**
TRUE ☐   FALSE ☐

3 **Whirlwind can control the sea and waves.**
TRUE ☐   FALSE ☐

4 Whirlwind can also heal injured friends.

TRUE ☐   FALSE ☐

5 Whirlwind first introduced Warnado to Master Eon.

TRUE ☐   FALSE ☐

6 Warnado gets dizzy when he spins around.

TRUE ☐   FALSE ☐

7 Warnado can pull his limbs and head inside his shell.

TRUE ☐   FALSE ☐

8 Sonic Boom's scream can knock foes flying.

TRUE ☐

FALSE ☐

MY SCORE /10

9 When an invisible wizard tried to steal Sonic Boom's eggs, she knew he was there because she smelled liver and Brussels sprouts.

TRUE ☐

FALSE ☐

10 Once her chicks hatch they grow to adult size in mere seconds.

TRUE ☐   FALSE ☐

ANSWERS

1 False. She's half-dragon, half-unicorn.

2 True. The Rainbow of Doom is pretty. Pretty terrifying that is!

3 False. Nope, it's the weather that obeys her commands.

4 True. As long as she's received the Rainbow of Healing.

5 True. She'd spotted the turtle twisting himself through Skylands.

6 False. He gets dizzy when he stands still!

7 True. It keeps him safe during a turtle slam.

8 True. And also friends if they get in the way. Watch your ears!

9 True. Most wizards can't get enough of the disgusting dish!

10 False. Because of the wizard's curse they return to their shells seconds after hatching.

LIGHTNING ROD

Are you the (h)airy action hero's number one fan?

1 **Complete the sentence: Lightning Rod is a Storm Giant, one of the . . .**
- **A** Oldest races in Skylands
- **B** Newest races to come to Skylands
- **C** Smelliest races in Skylands

2 **Where does Lightning Rod live?**
- **A** The Giant Kingdom
- **B** The Thunder Kingdom
- **C** The Cloud Kingdom

3 **How do Storm Giants spend their spare time?**
- **A** Knitting
- **B** Competing in athletic games
- **C** Sunbathing

4 **What does Lightning Rod wear on his wrists?**
- **A** Giant sweatbands, ideal for mopping up perspiration

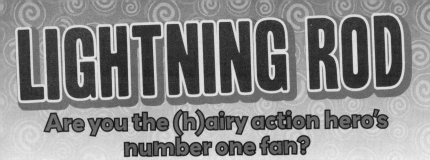

B Giant watches, ideal for seeing how long it is until tea time

C Giant copper bracelets, ideal for conducting electricity

5 **Lightning Rod was the 1000-metre lightning bolt hurl champion for over 200 years, until he had a little accident. What was it?**

A He slipped on his cloud and accidentally electrocuted his own beard

B Instead of snatching up a lightning bolt he grabbed a stray sheep and launched the unfortunate lamb into orbit

C One of his lightning bolts veered into the crowd, blasting an innocent cyclops who was queuing for hotdogs

6 **What tournament was Lightning Rod competing in when he was first spotted by Eon?**

A 400-ton bench press

B Thousand-metre lightning bolt hurl

C Tiddly-winks

7 **His life changed forever when what appeared in the sky above the Storm Giants' stadium?**

A Kaos' giant floating head

B Occulous

C Malefor the dragon

8 **What colour is Lightning Rod's magnificent beard?**
A Charcoal grey
B Striking gold
C Reddish-brown

9 **One of Lightning Rod's most impressive tricks is the Cloud Zapper Satellite upgrade. What does it do?**

A It teleports you into outer space
B It cleans your cloud so it's shiny and new again
C A protective cloud follows you around, zapping nearby enemies

10 **What sound can be heard for miles around during the Storm Giant Games?**
A Laughter
B Thunder
C High-pitched sirens

MY SCORE /10

WHAT'S THE QUESTION?

In this quiz you already have all the answers. You just need to find the right question!

 Laser beams.
- **A** What do Tech spell punks summon?
- **B** What do Air spell punks summon?
- **C** What do Life spell punks summon?

 Two.
- **A** How many bows does Flameslinger have?
- **B** How many shields does a Goliath Drow carry?
- **C** How many books are in Master Eon's library?

3 Crackling electricity.
- **A** How do windbag djinnis attack?
- **B** How do you destroy a Rotting Robbie?
- **C** What powers a Drow Zeppelin?

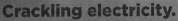

4 **Hob 'n' Yaros.**
A What is the name of Kaos' brothers?
B What is Ghost Roaster's real name?
C What is the name of the little red thieves that pinch things all over Skylands?

5 **In the waters around the ruins of Eon's Citadel.**
A Where is Kaos' secret base?
B Where did the Weapon Master go to sleep?
C Where was Camo born?

6 **They have no eyes.**
A Why are cyclopses smelly?
B Why don't zombies eat flesh?
C What's strange about Bone 'n' Arrow archers?

7 **A Mabu.**
A What is Snuckles?
B What is Gurglefin?
C What is Diggs?

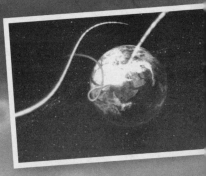

8 **Planet Earth.**
A To where did the Skylanders get banished?
B Where do rhu-babies come from?
C Where does Trigger Happy hide his gold?

9 **Black.**
  A What colour is the Skylands sun?
  B What colour are Hex's fingernails?
  C What colour is Eon's beard?

10 **Arkeyan Hammahs.**
  A What army did Chop Chop belong to?
  B What tools did the ancient Arkeyans use to build their war machines?
  C What is the name of the guards that protect Dragon's Peak?

MY SCORE /10

WORD WARRIORS

Skylander Search

Skylanders can be all kinds of weird and wonderful creatures. Can you find the 14 Skylands lifeforms in the grid? Plus, which creature appears twice?

Bambazookers
Dinosaurs
Dragons
Elves
Gillmen
Griffins
Lava creatures
Ooga orcs
Phoenix
Rock golems
Storm giants
Trees
Unicorns
Yeti

```
B I Q K O S D F X B G U X B S
G B A H E O L R Y O S N I A R
V D X V S I G J O T B I N M U
P S L A H N I A O I F C E B A
N E J F T M X R O V N O O A S
P T A B U T M P A R D R H Z O
S M E L O G K C O R C N P O N
D A Y T I J D T R E E S K O I
L A V A C R E A T U R E S K D
U Y N P A Z L K X U Y K S E J
M T E G F G R I F F I N S R M
S V O T E K H O Y I X R W S X
M N J T I P G N E Z M U L C W
S N E M L L I G V B I Y O M P
V A V O J J B G S N O G A R D
```

The creature that appears twice is:

MY
SCORE
/15

Kriss Kross

See if you can fit all of these Skylanders into the grid. To help get you started, Prism Break's name has already been filled in.

4 Letters
Zook

5 letters
Spyro

6 letters
Boomer
Cynder

7 letters
Eruptor
Sunburn
Ignitor

8 letters
Terrafin

9 letters
Sonic Boom

10 letters
~~Prism Break~~
Stump Smash
Stealth Elf

MY
SCORE

/12

PRISMBREAK

sunburn

ZOOK

For an extra point, rearrange the letters in the shaded squares to spell out the name of another Skylander:

_ _ _ _   _ _ _

Skylander Search

```
B I Q K O S D F X B G U X B S
G B A H E O L R Y O S N I A R
V D X V S I G J O T B I N M U
P S L A H N I A O I F C E B A
N E J F T M X R O V N O O A S
P T A B U T M P A R D R H Z O
S M E L O G K C O R C N P O N
D A Y T I J D T R E E S K O I
L A V A C R E A T U R E S K D
U Y N P A Z L K X U Y K S E J
M T E G F G R I F F I N S R M
S V O T E K H O Y I X R W S X
M N J T I P G N E Z M U L C W
S N E M L L I G V B I Y O M P
V A V O J J B G S N O G A R D
```

Dragons are listed twice.

Kriss Cross

The other Skylander is **Slam Bam**.

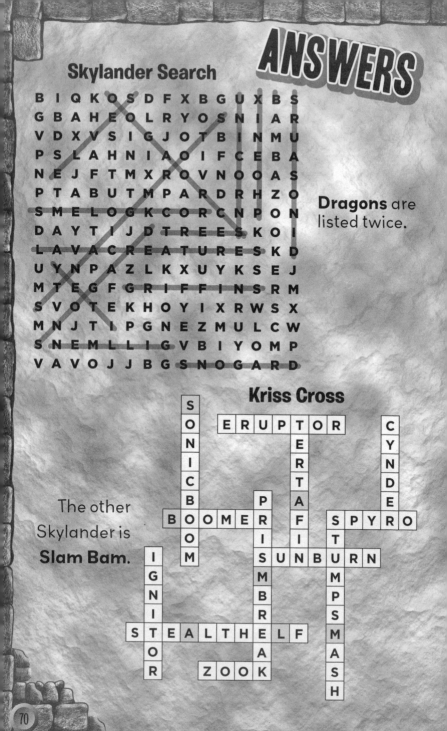

```
S
O   E R U P T O R                 C
N               E                 Y
I               R                 N
C               T                 D
B         P     A                 E
B O O M E R I   F     S P Y R O
O         R     I     T
M         S U N B U R N
I     P   M           U
G     R   B           M
N     I   R           P
S T E A L T H E L F   S
O     I   A           M
R     Z O O K         A
                      S
                      H
```

THE LIFE ELEMENT

Ten questions about Skylands' natural heroes

1 **What is Zook?**
- **A** A Nuttjobian
- **B** A Bambazooker
- **C** A Fast Reeder

2 **Why didn't Zook's people ever leave their muddy home?**
- **A** Master Eon told them to stay put
- **B** They were all asleep
- **C** They didn't know they could walk

3 **Zook's bamboo tube makes a mean bazooka, but what musical instrument can it double as?**
- **A** A didgeridoo
- **B** A flute
- **C** An E-flat double bass

4 **Which of these isn't one of Zook's upgrades?**

A Foliage Fungi

B Fightin' Foliage

C Fungal Bloom

5 **Which of these statements about Stealth Elf's origins is true?**

A She is Stump Smash's daughter

B Her best friend as a child was a prince called Kaos

C She awoke one morning in a hollow tree, with no memory of where she came from

6 **Who was Stealth Elf trained by?**

A A troll assassin

B A tree ninja

C A squirrel spy

7 **Complete the sentence: To confuse enemies, Stealth Elf . . .**

A . . . disguises herself as a green version of Kaos himself

B . . . transforms herself into a potted plant

C . . . creates duplicate decoys of herself

8 Where was Camo born?
A In Master Eon's vegetable patch
B By the roots of the Tree of life
C In a Skylands bamboo forest

9 Camo can create what type of exploding fruit?
A Melons
B Mangos
C Pomegranates

10 When he's not battling evil, Camo likes to spend his time doing what?
A Carving sweet potatoes and kumquats into comical effigies of Kaos
B Judging the cyclopses' annual novelty vegetable growing competition
C Tending Eon's vegetable garden

MY SCORE
/10

STUMP SMASH

1 When Stump Smash snoozes he can sleep through just about anything. Once, he woke from a nice long nap to find that the forest around him had been cut down.

TRUE ☐   FALSE ☐

2 His family of trees were felled by a team of lumberjack Mabu.

TRUE ☐   FALSE ☐

3 He was so angry that his branches all fell off in fury.

TRUE ☐   FALSE ☐

4 Stump Smash has more than just massive mallet hands to defend himself. He can also spit gob-tastic acorns at his enemies.

TRUE ☐

FALSE ☐

5 Once he had finished pile-driving the fiends who cut down his home, Stump Smash decided to side with that bald bandit, Kaos.

TRUE ☐   FALSE ☐

6 Even though this all happened a long time ago, Stump Smash is still a grumpy so and so.

TRUE ☐   FALSE ☐

7 Even though he's really heavy, Stump Smash can float in water.

TRUE ☐ FALSE ☐

8 Stump Smash's acorns always remain smooth as pebbles.

TRUE ☐ FALSE ☐

9 Over the years, Stump Smash has grown to love trolls and their pesky ways.

TRUE ☐ FALSE ☐

10 His battle cry is 'Slam Dunk!'

TRUE ☐ FALSE ☐

MY SCORE /10

ANSWERS

1 True. His snoring must have covered up the noise of the logging machines!

2 False. It was lumberjack trolls!

3 False. The trolls had cut off his branches too! The rotters.

4 True. And they're as hard as rocks. Acorns away!

5 False. Perish the thought. He sought out Eon to join the fight against the Darkness.

6 True. But his bark is much worse than his bite.

7 True. As long as he has the Waterlogged Super Upgrade.

8 False. Upgrading his abilities can make them super spiky. Ouch!

9 False. To this day, they make his bark crawl.

10 False. It's 'Drop the Hammer!'.

WEAPONS AT THE READY

Match the weapon to the Skylander

1 **Dragonfang Daggers**
- **A** Chop Chop
- **B** Stealth Elf
- **C** Cynder

2 **Phantom Orb**
- **A** Voodood
- **B** Dark Spyro
- **C** Hex

3 **Bamboo Bazooka**
- **A** Zook
- **B** Gill Grunt
- **C** Double Trouble

4 Mega Blasters
A Drobot
B Prism Break
C Wham-Shell

5 Flame Blade
A Eruptor
B Sunburn
C Ignitor

6 Drill Rocket
A Lightning Rod
B Drill Sergeant
C Wrecking Ball

7 Arkeyan Blade
A Warnado
B Chop Chop
C Whirlwind

8 Chain Whip
A Dino-Rang
B Whirlwind
C Ghost Roaster

9 Golden Pistols
A Terrafin
B Spyro
C Trigger Happy

10 Dynamite
A Boomer
B Slam Bam
C Camo

MY SCORE /10

ANSWERS

1 B
2 C
3 A
4 B
5 C

6 B
7 B
8 C
9 C
10 A

WORD WARRIORS

Pathfinder

Can you find a path through this grid, using all the words listed below? You can move up, down or sideways, but never diagonally. When you've finished, you'll have used up all but six of the squares.

Hugo has found the first word for you...

TRIGGER HAPPY

SPYRO

SPIDERS

SEADOG

RHUBARBS

PERSEPHONE

OCCULOUS

NORT

IMP

HYDRA

FLAMESLINGER

ELF

BASH

ARKEYAN

YETI

MY SCORE

/15

B	A	Y	D	A	N	O	E	R
C	S	H	R	Y	T	R	G	H
I	P	Y	A	E	R	I	G	A
D	S	U	R	K	N	Y	P	P
E	R	O	P	E	S	E	T	I
G	S	L	H	D	R	E	P	M
O	E	U	O	N	E	L	F	E
D	A	C	A	B	G	N	L	A
R	O	C	R	U	E	I	R	M
Y	P	S	B	H	R	L	S	E

The extra letters spell out the name of a Skylander with a dark past. Write it here:

Match Blocks

A challenge has been issued! Put each block from group A in front of a different block from group B to make eight four-letter names. Hugo has done the first one for you, matching BA and SH to make BASH.

A	B		A	B
			BA	SH

MY
SCORE

/8

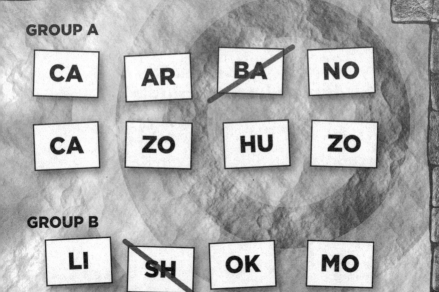

CA · AR · ~~BA~~ · NO

CA · ZO · HU · ZO

GROUP B

LI · ~~SH~~ · OK · MO

GO · RT · OS · BO

Riddle-me-ree

Can you work out the identity of this Skylander from the riddle?

My **first** is in BEACH and also in SEA

My **second** is in DOOR but not in KEY

My **third** is in UDDER though not in COW

My **fourth** is in POW but not in WOW

My **fifth** is in TREE although not in BARK

My **sixth** is in DOOM but not in DARK

My **seventh** is in RISE as well as GROW

My **whole** is a hot-head who is ready to BLOW

Answer:

MY SCORE

/1

ANSWERS

Pathfinder

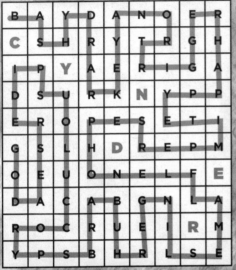

B	A	Y	D	A	N	O	E	R
C	S	H	R	Y	T	R	G	H
I	P	Y	A	E	R	I	G	A
D	S	U	R	K	N	Y	P	P
E	R	O	P	E	S	E	T	I
G	S	L	H	D	R	E	P	M
O	E	U	O	N	E	L	F	E
D	A	C	A	B	G	N	L	A
R	O	C	R	U	E	I	R	M
Y	P	S	B	H	R	L	S	E

The hidden
name is:
Cynder

Match Blocks

A	B		A	B
CA	LI		HU	GO
AR	BO		CA	MO
ZO	OK		BA	SH
KA	OS		NO	RT

Riddle-me-ree
Eruptor

85

KAOS' MIND-MELTING QUIZZES OF DOOM!

BWAHAHAHAHA!

Oh, look, it's one of Eon's precious Portal Pretenders. On a Quiz Quest, are you? Then you've just run out of luck, FOOLISH FOOL!

Why? Because I'M the Quiz Master now! Prepare to be confounded by my calamitous conundrums! Baffled by my baleful brain-teasers. Perplexed by my putrefying puzzles!

You're doomed, I tell you. DOOOOOMED!

Kaos

P.S. Have I mentioned that you're doomed?

ULTIMATE KAOS

Glumshanks has set ten killer questions about yours truly. You'll never be able to answer them. NEVER!

1 Master Kaos didn't always know that he was a Portal Master. What was he before he became an evil genius?
- **A** A servant boy
- **B** A royal prince
- **C** A Skylander

2 What colour are Master Kaos' eyes?
- **A** Beastly blue
- **B** Revolting red
- **C** Gruesome green

3 Why did Master Kaos leave the royal palace and set out on his own?
- **A** He was fed up with being teased for being bald, ugly and smelling like cabbage
- **B** He was banished by his father after he blew up the royal guinea pig (accidentally, of course)
- **C** He wanted to meet his hero, Eon

4 **How did he meet his faithful and loyal sidekick Glumshanks?**

A He found Glumshanks being menaced by a cactus monster in the Dirt Seas

B They met at the annual 'Young Tyrant of the Year' competition

C Glumshanks was his butler back in their palace days

5 **After leaving the royal palace, Master Kaos found it difficult to find friends*, so he used his magic power to make his own. What were they called?**

A The Wilikin

B The Manikin

C The Twiggikin

6 **What were these new friends actually made from?**

A Worms   **B** Wood   **C** Wool

7 **Why doesn't Master Kaos like trees?**

A They remind him of his father

B He is allergic to leaves

C He believes they are plotting against him

* Friends!? Pah! Who needs 'em when you have minions?

8 **Which foolish creatures rejected Master Kaos' kind and generous offer to join his minions?**
   A The gremlins
   B The storm giants
   C The lava kings

9 **Master Kaos was once banished to a distant place. Where was it?**
   A The South Pole
   B The Outlands
   C The naughty step

10 **What does Master Kaos hide behind when he goes into battle?****
   A A giant, floating head
   B A giant, floating knee
   C Glumshanks

MY SCORE
/10

** Hide? Kaos doesn't hide! How dare you Glumshanks! Just wait until I get you home!

90

MEMORY BUSTER

When I'm bored, I pass the time by writing down lists of things I hate! I've filled 73 books with them now. Here are my top ten. Gaze at them with your horrible eyes for a few minutes, and then turn to page 101.

I bet you can't write them down from memory in the right order!

1 The Core of Light
2 Spyro
3 Eon
4 Trees
5 Soap
6 Hair
7 Beards
8 Flowers
9 Kittens
10 Herbal tea

TROLLS ON PARADE

Ah, my troll hordes. Loyal, ruthless and largely stupid. How they adore me! Draw a line to link the type of trolls and weapons to the right descriptions.

1 Wearing spiked helmets, these trolls love to chuck bombs at anything that moves.

2 A tank that trudges along on two legs.

3 Aggressive little bruisers who will pummel you with their heavy tools.

4 Ouch. The sharp claws of these trolls are razor sharp – maybe even sharper!

5 Take aim! These gun-carrying trolls have you in their sights!

6 The troll's finest mechanical achievement. Driven by grease-monkeys and armed with twin cannons. Fire!

A Blaster trolls

B Troll greasemonkeys

C Trollverine

D Mark 31 troll tank

E Troll grenadier

F Gun snout

MY
SCORE
/6

CYCLOPS
True or False

Eye eye, here are ten cyclopean conundrums for you. See what I did there? 'Eye eye'! Cyclops! Hah, I'm hilarious! (Why is no one laughing?)

1 Cyclopses smell of lovely perfume.
TRUE ☐   FALSE ☐

2 Furyclops wear novelty reindeer antlers.
TRUE ☐
FALSE ☐

3 Cyclops choppers are invulnerable while spinning.
TRUE ☐
FALSE ☐

4 Cyclopess are master stonemasons.
TRUE ☐   FALSE ☐

5 The cyclopses that dwell near the valley of Vindlevale are known as snowclopses.
TRUE ☐   FALSE ☐

6 Uniquely, cyclops chuckers have two eyes.
TRUE ☐   FALSE ☐

7 Timidclopses roll explosive boulders at their enemies.
TRUE ☐   FALSE ☐

8 Cyclops mammoths have unusually small paws.

TRUE ☐

FALSE ☐

9 The cyclopses' greatest achievement was carving the stone ships of the Cyclops Navy.

TRUE ☐   FALSE ☐

10 Cyclops chuckers are bigger than timidclops.

TRUE ☐   FALSE ☐

MY SCORE

/10

COUNTDOWN

Count the number of times these letters are repeated to spell out the name of a toothy beast ...
a toothy beast OF DOOOOOM!

MY SCORE

/1

1	5	2	4	3	8	6	3	7

EVIL WORDSEARCH

HA HA! I have unleashed my evil minions into this gruesome grid of gargantuan proportions. Find them, if you DARE!

DARK IMP
PYRO ARCHER
DOOMSHARK
EVIL ENT
NINJA MINION
WATER DRAGON
ICE YETI
KNIGHT
MISSILE MINION
PHOENIX DRAGON

To make it even more difficult for you, Portal Poser, one of these minions is missing from the grid. You'll never be able to tell me which one it is. Bwaha-HA!

```
N D X I G Z M L S F N C Y N M
T O O K H Z Q N L O J G T O Z
I H I O Q E S X I K E K Y G X
C Q G N M I K N C V S Q K A O
E D D I I S I U I W A B H R X
Y Q K D N M H L Y X R C Y D T
E Y I F A K E A B X D E K X J
T H K J V N Z L R C C Q G I N
I M N W T P P M I K R A D N M
Y I P D M I B F E S X T K E F
N C O A R E D B F T S V T O A
Z P Y R O A R C H E R I R H B
Z O U N K F E G P O N K M P A
X F R K J Y C M Q G E L I K E
I F N U Y G Z V P C E L V V D
```

The missing minion is:

MY SCORE

/10

Evil Wordsearch

```
N D X I G Z M L S F N C Y N M
T O O K H Z Q N L O J G T O Z
I H I O Q E S X I K E K Y G X
C Q G N M I K N C V S Q K A O
E D D I I S I U I W A B H R X
Y Q K D N M H L Y X R C Y D T
E Y I F A K E A B X D E K X J
T H K J V N Z L R C C Q G I N
I M N W T P P M I K R A D N M
Y I P D M I B F E S X T K E F
N C O A R E D B F T S V T O A
Z P Y R O A R C H E R I R H B
Z O U N K F E G P O N K M P A
X F R K J Y C M Q G E L I K E
I F N U Y G Z V P C E L V V D
```

The missing minion is the **Water Dragon.**
I can't believe you got that one right!

Countdown

1	5	2	4	3	8	6	3	7
L	E	V	I	A	T	H	A	N

MEMORY BUSTER

See if you can write down my list of things I despise from page 91 – in the right order, mind! And no peeking! I hate cheats (Drat! Forgot to put them on my list!).

1.

2.

3.

4.

5.

6.

7.

8.

9.

10.

Score
You get one point for each one you remember, and another point for each one you get in the right order.

MY SCORE
/20

BEWARE THE MINIONS OF KAOS!

So you think you're clever, do you? Think again. I – Kaos – summon my "UNANSWERABLE QUESTIONS OF ULTIMATE DIFFICULTNESS"!

1 **What are the Drow?**
A Evil trolls
B Evil elves
C Evil Mabu

2 **Undead spell punks can summon which evil creatures?**
- **A** Rhu-babies
- **B** Rotting Robbies
- **C** Stump demons

3 **Where did the trolls live before they worked for Kaos?**
- **A** Under cabbage patches
- **B** Under paving slabs
- **C** Under bridges

4 **What are Drow airships called?**
- **A** Zeppelins
- **B** Blimps
- **C** Deathballoons

5 How many claws do cyclops mammoths have on each foot?

A 2
B 3
C 4

6 Trolls like to play fetch with chompies using lit dynamite. What do they call this game?

A Fetch!
B Go-get-it!
C Boom!

7 What is mounted on the end of a Drow Spearman's weapon?

A A blade
B A star
C A sheep

8 **What do Blitzer Bullies carry on their backs?**
- **A** Tech spell punks
- **B** Life spell punks
- **C** Fire spell punks

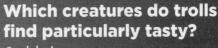

9 **What do Drow Witches throw?**
- **A** Tantrums
- **B** Razor-sharp flying discs
- **C** Enchanted mud pies

10 **Which creatures do trolls find particularly tasty?**
- **A** Unicorns
- **B** Dragons
- **C** Gillmen

MY SCORE /10

105

THE UNDEAD ELEMENT

True or False – time to get spooky!

1 **Chop Chop was an Arkeyan wizard.**
TRUE ☐ FALSE ☐

2 **Chop Chop's steel blade is completely indestructible.**
TRUE ☐ FALSE ☐

3 **Chop Chop was discovered in a crumbling crypt by Glumshanks' explorer uncle, Mopeshanks.**
TRUE ☐
FALSE ☐

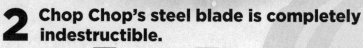

4 Cynder is the daughter of the evil dragon Malefor.

TRUE ☐ FALSE ☐

5 When she was younger, Cynder terrorized the residents of her homeland.

TRUE ☐ FALSE ☐

6 Cynder changed her ways after she was defeated by Hex.

TRUE ☐ FALSE ☐

7 Cynder can summon ghosts from beyond the grave.

TRUE ☐ FALSE ☐

8 Before he was transformed into an Undead demon, Ghost Roaster was a chef.

TRUE ☐ FALSE ☐

9 Master Eon chained Ghost Roaster to a spiked metal ball in punishment for his crimes.

TRUE ☐

FALSE ☐

10 Ghost Roaster's teeth may be pin-sharp, but his skull-like head is surprisingly soft.

TRUE ☐ FALSE ☐

MY SCORE /10

ANSWERS

1 False. He was a member of the Arkeyan Elite Guard.

2 True. Those Arkeyans certainly knew how to forge weapons.

3 False. He was found by Master Eon.

4 False. One of Malefor's henchmen stole Cynder from her mother when she was still in her egg.

5 True. But in her heart she knew it was wrong.

6 False. She was bested by none other than Spyro!

7 True. When she goes into a Shadow Dash they manifest in her wake.

8 True. His name was Olav and his speciality was sheep-wool stew. Yum!

9 False. It was a spectral ruler who punished Ghost Roaster for eating all his phantom subjects.

10 False. It's a skull-butting battering ram!

HEX

Do you know the secrets of the spooky Skylands sorceress?

1 What was Hex before she became one of the Undead?
- **A** A Mabu
- **B** An elf
- **C** A troll

2 Why did the Undead dragon king Malefor want to capture her?
- **A** She was the most powerful sorceress in all of Skylands
- **B** He fell in love with her
- **C** She made amazing sheep trotter and cabbage pies

3 How did Hex first respond to Malefor's plan to kidnap her?
- **A** She kidnapped him first
- **B** She went into hiding with the other wizards, witches and soothsayers of the realm
- **C** She asked Eon to send the Skylanders after the Dragon King

4 **How did she join the leagues of the Undead?**

A She asked Kaos to turn her into an Undead sorceress so she could defeat Malefor

B She ate a bowl of Ghost Roaster's ghoulash (made with real ghouls) by mistake

C She descended into the Valley of the Undead to face Malefor and was immediately transformed

5 **What happened when she blasted Malefor with her most apocalyptic spell?**

A When the smoke cleared, Malefor had been turned into a statue

B When the smoke cleared, she found herself back in her home village

C When the smoke cleared, Malefor was twice his normal size

6 **Why are some inhabitants of Skylands still wary of Hex?**

A They suspect she has used her sorcery skills for evil purposes

B They suspect she's in league with the sheep

C They suspect she's actually Kaos in disguise

7 What colour is Hex's skin now that she is undead?

A Gruesome green
B Ghastly red
C Ghostly blue

8 To protect herself, Hex can conjure up . . .

A A wall of tombstones
B A wall of bones
C A wall of chains

9 Which one of the following <u>isn't</u> one of Hex's upgrades?

A Unstable Phantom Orbs
B Caustic Phantom Orbs
C Explosive Phantom Orbs

10 Hex can summon some pretty weird weather. What rains down when she casts a spell?

A Skulls
B Toads
C Jellyfish

MY
SCORE
/10

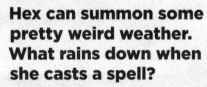

ANSWERS

1 B
2 A
3 B
4 C
5 B

6 A
7 C
8 B
9 C
10 A

111

ANAGRAMANIA!

Rearrange the letters to solve the anagrams and find the Skylanders!

1 **Bawling Clerk**
Hint: It's a Magic Skylander

2 **Shawl Helm**
Hint: It's a Water Skylander

3 **Harpy Get Grip**
Hint: It's a Tech Skylander

4 Smellier Fang
Hint: It's a Fire Skylander

5 Mass Thumps
Hint: It's a Life Skylander

6 Sort Shortage
Hint: It's an Undead Skylander

7 Hit Long Grind
Hint: It's an Air Skylander

8 On Daring
Hint: It's an Earth Skylander

9 Danger Trellis
Hint: It's another Tech Skylander

10 Mere as Not
Hint: It's not a Skylander at all.
Sneaky old me!

MY SCORE

/10

ANSWERS

1	Wrecking Ball	6	Ghost Roaster
2	Wham-Shell	7	Lightning Rod
3	Trigger Happy	8	Dino-Rang
4	Flameslinger	9	Drill Sergeant
5	Stump Smash	10	Master Eon

PICTURE PUZZLES

Count the Symbols

How many Elements symbols are clustered on this page? Write the totals in the boxes at the bottom.

MY SCORE

/4

⬡ =

◎ =

✿ =

✦ =

Odd One Out

Which one of these Skylanders doesn't belong in the group?

MY
SCORE

/1

Shadow Dragon

Only one of these
shadows perfectly
matches Camo,
but which
is it?

A

B

MY
SCORE
/1

Slice 'n' Dice

Which three Skylanders can you see in this picture?

ANSWERS

Count the symbols

Odd one out

Chop Chop – he's from the Undead Element. The others are all Tech.

Shadow Dragon

Only shadow F is a perfect match

Slice 'n' Dice

Trigger Happy, Whirlwind, Hex

MY SCORE /3

121

THE EARTH ELEMENT

Get to grips with the most down-to-Earth Skylanders around.

1 **Bash is an unusual type of dragon. What is different about him?**
- **A** He is allergic to fire
- **B** He is wingless
- **C** He can turn into a butterfly

2 **How does Bash get around?**
- **A** He hops like a bulky, brawny bunny
- **B** He burrows beneath the ground
- **C** He rolls himself into a rocky ball

3 **How far can Bash swing his tail?**
- **A** 360 degrees
- **B** 180 degrees
- **C** 90 degrees

4 **What is Dino-Rang?**
- **A** A dragon
- **B** An ogre
- **C** A dinosaur

5 **When hunters tried to snaffle away his flock, how did Bash rescue his brothers and sisters?**

A He disguised himself as a hunter and snuck on board the hunter's ship

B He launched himself through the hull of the hunter's ship like a cannonball

C He grabbed hold of the anchor of the hunter's ship and pulled it back to earth

6 **Why does Dino-Rang search for the fabled Twin Diamond Boomerangs?**

A He believes they will take him home – wherever that is

B He loves shiny things

C They will give him huge, leathery wings like a pterodactyl

7 **Which of the following isn't one of Dino-Rang's upgrades?**

A Volcanic Glass Boomerangs

B Stellar Boomerangs

C Dancing Boomerangs

8 Prism Break is a golem, but what kind of golem is he?

A Rock

B Mustard

C Cardboard

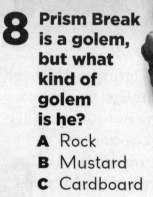

9 When Prism Break fell asleep in his mine, he was caught in a cave-in. How long was he trapped underground?

A 50 years   **B** 100 years   **C** 1000 years

10 Who found Prism Break in his subterranean prison?

A Mabu miners

B Troll tunnellers

C Cyclops cavers

MY SCORE

/10

TERRAFIN

True or False – just when you thought it was safe to answer more questions...

1 Terrafin spent his youth in the Deep Blue Sea.

TRUE ☐ FALSE ☐

2 Before he was a Skylander, he was a pirate.

TRUE ☐ FALSE ☐

3 One fateful day a mysterious explosion in the sky turned his home into a giant sheet of glass.

TRUE ☐ FALSE ☐

4 After he rescued everyone from the explosion, Terrafin trained to be a seafood chef.

TRUE ☐   FALSE ☐

5 Terrafin can 'swim' through the earth.

TRUE ☐   FALSE ☐

6 Terrafin has never won a fight.

TRUE ☐   FALSE ☐

7 Terrafin has orange and yellow bumps on his back.

TRUE ☐   FALSE ☐

8 With one of his upgrades, Terrafin gets punchy golden knuckles.

TRUE ☐

FALSE ☐

9 Terrafin discovered Drill Sergeant.

TRUE ☐   FALSE ☐

10 When Kaos was banished to the Outlands he owed Terrafin five dollars.

TRUE ☐   FALSE ☐

MY SCORE

/10

127

WHO'S WHO?

Eon knows his Skylanders like the back of his hand (like the back of both of them, in fact). But do you? Who is he describing here?

1 **A skeletal warrior who loves following orders.**
- **A** Voodood
- **B** Chop Chop
- **C** Ghost Roaster

2 **A brave soul who can harness dark Magic to become even more powerful.**
- **A** Hex
- **B** Legendary Trigger Happy
- **C** Dark Spyro

3 An agile and speedy fighter, skilled beyond her years.
- **A** Stealth Elf
- **B** Ignitor
- **C** Sonic Boom

4 Ferocious, stormy and wild, but pure of heart.
- **A** Eruptor
- **B** Whirlwind
- **C** Stump Smash

5 She may have a shady past, but now she fights for good.
- **A** Eruptor
- **B** Sunburn
- **C** Cynder

6 Mysterious, serious and powerful, but always trustworthy.
- **A** Hex
- **B** Double Trouble
- **C** Wrecking Ball

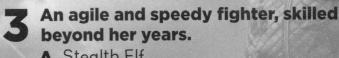

7 **A determined dragon who loves to roll with it.**
A Spyro   **B** Bash   **C** Zap

8 **A charming and charismatic champion who is a hero to many.**
A Lightning Rod
B Trigger Happy
C Drobot

9 **Artistic and a bit of a loner, but always armed for battle.**
A Prism Break
B Terrafin
C Slam Bam

10 **Always hungry and with a destructive streak.**
A Wrecking Ball
B Dino-Rang
C Eruptor

11
A juggernaut of a Skylander, loyal and obedient.
- **A** Gill Grunt
- **B** Drill Sergeant
- **C** Boomer

12
A determined, hyper-intelligent inventor.
- **A** Boomer
- **B** Flameslinger
- **C** Drobot

13
Explosive and energetic, this Skylander loves fruit.
- **A** Wham-Shell
- **B** Camo
- **C** Zook

MY SCORE /13

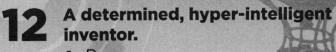

ANSWERS

1 B	**5** C	**9** C			
2 C	**6** A	**10** A			
3 A	**7** B	**11** B			
4 B	**8** A	**12** C			
		13 B			

131

ARMED AND DANGEROUS

Which weapons or attacks belong to these Skylanders?

1 Gill Grunt
- **A** Harpoon Gun
- **B** Troll Bomb
- **C** Scorching Blade

2 Trigger Happy
- **A** Dendrite Focus Crystals
- **B** Golden Machine Gun
- **C** Tiki Tiki Staff

3 Stealth Elf
A Elven Spinblade
B Legendary Blade
C Arkeyan Vorpal Blade

4 Stump Smash
A Power Hose
B Bazooka
C Meganut

5 Drill Sergeant
A Arkeyan Spectral Shield
B Auto-blaster
C Galvanized Bladegears

6 Chop Chop
A Bone Brambler
B MIRV Drill Rockets
C Inferno Blade

7 Camo
A Black Lightning
B Triple Bundle Dynamite
C Sunburst

8 Drobot
A Antimatter Charges
B Searing Sun Blast
C Golden Pistols

9 Wham-Shell
A Axon Focus Crystals
B Electro Axe
C Malacostracan Mace

10 Flameslinger
A Searing Arrows
B Tri-Spread Bladegears
C Chain Whip

ANSWERS

1 A
2 B
3 A
4 C
5 B

6 A
7 C
8 A
9 C
10 A

MY SCORE /10

THE TECH ELEMENT

True or False – test yourself on the technology-loving titans.

1 Drobot couldn't fly at all when he was young.

TRUE ☐

FALSE ☐

2 A Tech spell punk created Drobot's robot armour.

TRUE ☐ FALSE ☐

3 Drobot's voice synthesizer gives him a deep, booming voice.

TRUE ☐ FALSE ☐

4 Drill Sergeant was built by the Ancient Benevolents.

TRUE ☐   FALSE ☐

5 Upon his discovery, a grateful Drill Sergeant swore allegiance to the Skylander who found him.

TRUE ☐   FALSE ☐

6 The first order he received from the Skylander was "make me a cup of tea!"

TRUE ☐   FALSE ☐

7 Drill Sergeant can fire his drillbits like rockets.

TRUE ☐   FALSE ☐

8 When he was little, Boomer liked to blow up cows.

TRUE ☐   FALSE ☐

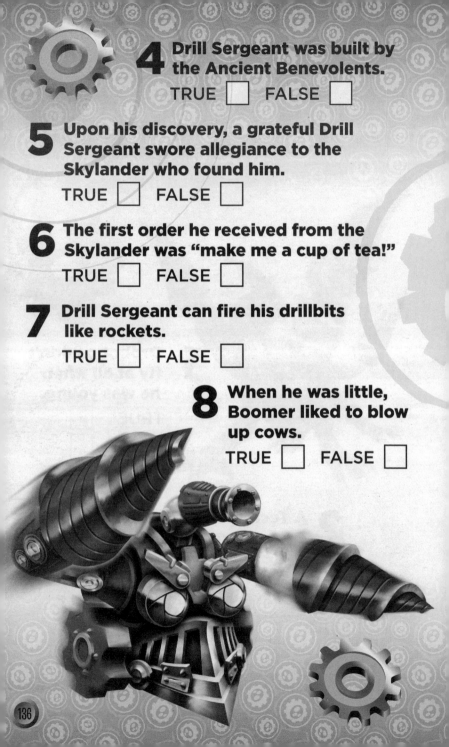

9 Boomer was once a member of the troll army.

TRUE ☐

FALSE ☐

10 Boomer can create shuddering shockwaves by smashing his gauntlets into the ground.

TRUE ☐   FALSE ☐

MY SCORE /10

137

TRIGGER HAPPY

Set your sights on answering these questions.

1 **What kind of tricky critter is Trigger Happy?**

A A goblin

B A gremlin

C A gorgon

2 **When did Trigger Happy first turn up in Skylands?**

A When Kaos destroyed the Core of Light

B When the Arkeyans were banished

C When a group of bandits were menacing a frontier island town

3 **How did Trigger Happy see off the dastardly bandits?**
- **A** He stole their dragon steeds from outside the bank
- **B** He opened fire on them with solid gold coins
- **C** He convinced townsfolk to form a posse and fight back

4 **What happened to the gold coins that Trigger Happy fired at the bandits?**
- **A** They transformed into sapphire diamonds
- **B** He let the townsfolk keep them and they became rich overnight
- **C** The bandits nicked 'em

5 **What is Trigger Happy's favourite solution to any problem?**
- **A** Calmly discuss every possible option
- **B** Hide his head in the sand
- **C** Shoot something

6 How many toes does Trigger Happy have?

A None   B Six   C Twelve

7 What else is unusual about Trigger Happy?

A He's actually allergic to gold
B He has seven toes on each foot
C He has an extraordinarily long tongue

8 As well as firing golden coin bullets, what can Trigger Happy lob at his targets?

A Silver coins
B Gold safes
C Gold teeth

9 What is Trigger Happy's Super Upgrade called?

A Infinite Ammo
B Ultimate Ammo
C Unlimited Ammo

10 How many guns does Trigger Happy carry?

A One   B Two   C Three

MY SCORE /10

THE ARKEYANS

How well do you know your ancient Arkeyan history?

1 **Who were the Arkeyans?**
A The original Skylanders
B Ancient rulers of Skylands
C Kaos' second cousins twice removed

2 **Where did the Arkeyans live?**
A In vast cities under the ground
B In vast cities in the sky
C In vast cities above the ground

3 **What did they combine with magic to protect Skylands from the Darkness?**
A Plants
B Sheep
C Technology

4 **What was the name of the Arkeyan capital city?**
A The Royal City of Arkey
B The Royal City of Arko
C The Royal City of Arkus

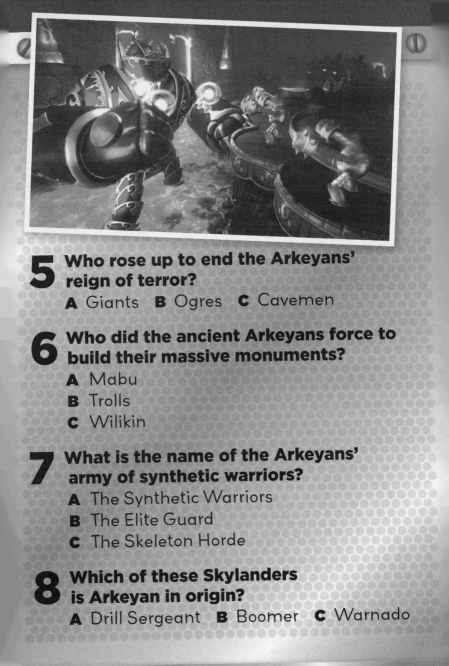

5 Who rose up to end the Arkeyans' reign of terror?

A Giants B Ogres C Cavemen

6 Who did the ancient Arkeyans force to build their massive monuments?

A Mabu

B Trolls

C Wilikin

7 What is the name of the Arkeyans' army of synthetic warriors?

A The Synthetic Warriors

B The Elite Guard

C The Skeleton Horde

8 Which of these Skylanders is Arkeyan in origin?

A Drill Sergeant B Boomer C Warnado

9 **What was special about the statue that stood in the waters around Eon's Citadel?**
- **A** It was a sleeping Arkeyan Weapon Master
- **B** It was Eon's lost long father
- **C** It was Eruptor dressed up as a statue for a surprise fancy dress party

10 **What do Arkeyan Control Towers actually Control?**
- **A** Arkeyan Hammahs
- **B** Arkeyan Defence Drones
- **C** Arkeyan Ultrons

MY SCORE

/10

ANSWERS

1 B	**5** A
2 A	**4** C
3 C	
6 A	
7 B	
8 A	
9 A	
10 B	

WORD WARRIORS

Search for the Elements

One Skylander from each of the eight Elements is hidden in the wordsearch opposite. Can you find them without a word list?

Magic ....

Water ....

Tech ....

Fire ....

Life ....

Undead ....

Earth ....

Air ....

Can you also find five of the Skylanders' greatest allies? Write their names below when you discover them.

....

....

....

....

....

T N R P O G U H M A A P E O D
L I O A O H Y A G P X H Z F O
Q F O C J H B S U N B U R N U
B A T F J M C I K P B I G W B
M R C A A G L P E A B F E S L
D R A L M L L R O E E L B N E
T E S Z U P S I V H U Y D O T
I T D G M E K U E W C N W E R
U N C R P T T Z U R F N F X O
H M Z H O Z U G D Y J G B J U
R V O I O B F Q Q X M C V Z B
T N B O I M O O B C I N O S L
E W K F B L F T H L Z S G P E
Y D L R S W A M K K L C R K L
D K U O G Y V C S G E Y O N F

MY **SCORE** /8

MY **SCORE** /5

145

Spiral

Write the answers to the questions in the grid. The last letter of one answer is the first of the next.

1   Trigger Happy's golden ammo of choice (5)

2   A toothy fish like Terrafin (5)

3   Skylands' number one villain. Boo. Hiss. (4)

4   A Corn Hornet has one of these on its tail (5)

5   A giant, black spider (10)

6   The weapon favoured by a cyclops chopper (3)

7   The answer to number three is definitely this, as are his minions (4)

8   One of the eight Elements (4)

9   What the Undead like to do to pies (3)

For an extra point, unscramble the letters in the shaded squares to find a legendary race of Skylanders.

Crazy Crossout

Cross out the letters that appear twice to reveal the name of a scary Skylander!

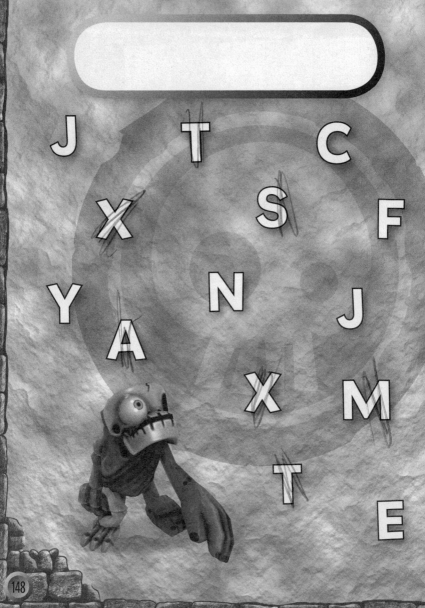

J T C

~~X~~ ~~S~~ F

Y ~~A~~ N J

~~X~~ M

~~T~~

E

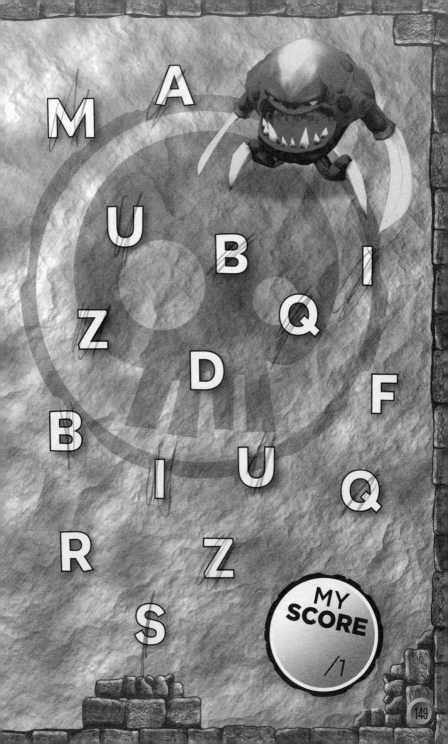

MY
SCORE
/1

149

Secret Friend

Solve the clues to reveal the name of a friend of the Skylanders in the shaded squares.

1 Prism Break has these instead of hands
2 Warnado is one
3 Hated by Gill Grunt
4 Wrecking Ball's super-long weapon
5 Lightning Rod's favourite thing to fling
6 Laid by Sonic Boom
7 Worn over Flameslinger's eyes
8 Terrafin's original home
9 Whirlwind has one

MY
SCORE
/9

ANSWERS

Search for the Elements

The Skylanders are:
DoubleTrouble, SlamBam,
Drobot, Sunburn, Zook, ChopChop,
Terrafin, SonicBoom.

The allies hidden in the grid are: Hugo, Flynn, Cali,
Eon, Persephone.

```
T N R P O G U H M A A P E O D
L I O A O H Y A G P X H Z F O
Q F O C J H B S U N B U R N U
B A T F J M C I K P B I G W B
M R C A A G L P E A B F E S L
D R A L M L L R O E E L B N E
T E S Z U P S I V H U Y D O T
I T D G M E K U E W C N W E R
U N C R P T T Z U R F N F X O
H M Z H O Z U G D Y J G B J U
R V O I O B F Q Q X M C V Z B
T N B O I M O O B C I N O S L
E W K F B L F T H L Z S G P E
Y D L R S W A M K K L C R K L
D K U O G Y V C S G E Y O N F
```

Spiral

The Legendary race of Skylanders is the GIANTS.

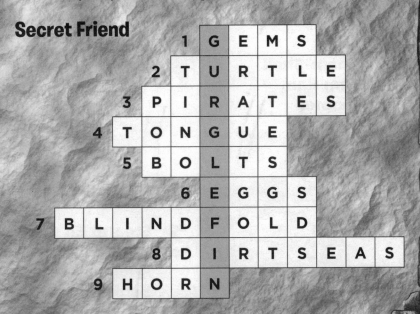

C	O	I	N	S	H	A	R
							K
A	X	E	V	I	L		A
L					I		O
U		T	A	E	F		S
T							T
N	A	G	R	A	G	N	I

Crazy Crossout

The scary Skylander is **Cynder**.

Secret Friend

#									
1		G	E	M	S				
2		T	U	R	T	L	E		
3		P	I	R	A	T	E	S	
4	T	O	N	G	U	E			
5		B	O	L	T	S			
6			E	G	G	S			
7	B	L	I	N	D	F	O	L	D
8			D	I	R	T	S	E	A	S
9		H	O	R	N				

153

ODD ONES OUT

In each group, can you find the Skylander who doesn't belong?

1 Spyro
Wrecking Ball
Voodood
Gill Grunt

2 Zap
Wham-Shell
Slam Bam
Boomer

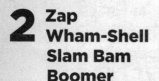

3 Stealth Elf
Eruptor
Ignitor
Sunburn

4 Stump Smash
Zook
Camo
Double Trouble

5 Ghost Roaster
Hex
Flameslinger
Cynder

6 Prism Break
Whirlwind
Bash
Terrafin

7 Sonic Boom, Warnado, Lightning Rod, Chop Chop

8 Dino-Rang, Drill Sergeant, Drobot, Trigger Happy

MY SCORE /8

ANSWERS

1 Gill Grunt. The rest are all Magic Skylanders.

2 Boomer. The rest are all Water Skylanders.

3 Stealth Elf. The rest are all Fire Skylanders.

4 Double Trouble. The rest are all Life Skylanders.

5 Flameslinger. The rest are all Undead Skylanders.

6 Whirlwind. The rest are all Earth Skylanders.

7 Chop Chop. The rest are all Air Skylanders.

8 Dino-Rang. The rest are all Tech Skylanders.

THAT'S NOT MY UPGRADE

Below are listed three upgrades for each of these Skylanders – but which doesn't belong to the hero in question? You get an extra point if you can name the Skylander the rogue upgrade belongs to!

1 **Whirlwind**
   A Rainbow Chain
   B Guided Twister
   C Tempest Tantrum

2 **Ghost Roaster**
   A Double Spooky
   B Phase Shift Burst
   C Unfinished Business

3 **Zook**
   A Full Splinter Jacket
   B Pollen Plume
   C Exploding Shrapnel

4 Drobot
- **A** Thruster Flight
- **B** Galvanized Bladegears
- **C** Mega Dozer

5 Spyro
- **A** The Daybringer Flame
- **B** Shaman Style
- **C** Comet Dash

6 Slam Bam
- **A** Blizzard Battle Armour
- **B** Poseidon Strike
- **C** Arctic Explosion

7 Eruptor
- **A** Incinerate
- **B** Fiery Remains
- **C** Magma Ball

8 Dino-Rang
- **A** Fist Trap Funeral
- **B** Basalt Boomerangs
- **C** Feeding Frenzy

MY
SCORE
/20

9 **Stealth Elf**
   A Ring of Might
   B Straw Pook Scarecrow
   C Elf Jitsu

10 **Chop Chop**
   A Demon Blade of the Underworld
   B Shield Stun Bash
   C Bone Fortress

ANSWERS

1 B - It belongs to Warnado.

2 A - It belongs to Cynder.

3 B - It belongs to Stump Smash.

4 C - It belongs to Drill Sergeant.

5 B - It belongs to Voodood.

6 B - It belongs to Wham-Shell.

7 A - It belongs to Ignitor.

8 C - It belongs to Terrafin.

9 A - It belongs to Camo.

10 C - It belongs to Hex.

PERSONALITY TEST

Match the Skylanders with the descriptions of their personalities.

1 Strong willed, young at heart and commanding.
- **A** Boomer
- **B** Spyro
- **C** Hex

2 Brave, righteous and with real fire in his belly.
- **A** Ignitor
- **B** Gill Grunt
- **C** Slam Bam

3 Speedy, talented and electrifying.
- **A** Voodood
- **B** Camo
- **C** Zap

4 Selfless, gifted and always on target.
   A Flameslinger
   B Cynder
   C Drill Sergeant

5 Big-hearted, determined and an old romantic.
   A Drobot
   B Trigger Happy
   C Gill Grunt

6 Brave, protective and maternal.
   A Sonic Boom
   B Ghost Roaster
   C Hex

7 Grumpy and vengeful – but loyal.
   A Warnado
   B Stump Smash
   C Wrecking Ball

8 **Unique, famous and a bit of a prankster.**
   A Dark Spyro
   B Sunburn
   C Wham-Shell

9 **Hot-headed and bad-tempered, but in control (most of the time).**
   A Bash   **B** Whirlwind   **C** Eruptor

10 **Obsessed with Magic, a bit of a loner and far from unique.**
   A Double Trouble
   B Chop Chop
   C Zook

11 Ruthless, lumbering and stony-faced.

A Prism Break
B Stealth Elf
C Stump Smash

12 A calm, optimistic hunter.

A Sunburn
B Dino-Rang
C Gill Grunt

13 Protective, determined and a bit of a brawler.

A Drill Sergeant
B Hex
C Terrafin

MY SCORE /13

UNDEAD FUNNY

Hmmmm. The Undead Skylanders struggle with humour at the best of times. They've managed to mix up these rib ticklers. Can you connect the right punchline to the right joke?

1 What's Chop Chop's favourite musical instrument?

2 What do young Rotting Robbies play?

3 What does Ghost Roaster serve for dessert?

4 Why did the cyclops have to close his school?

5 What kind of mail does Ghost Roaster send?

6 What do you get if you cross Slam Bam and Hex?

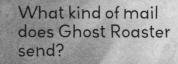

A Corpses and robbers!

B He only had one pupil!

C A trom-bone!

D Chain letters!

E A cold spell!

F Ice scream!

MY
SCORE
/6

BLITZED
BATTLE CRIES

The Skylanders have got tongue-tied. Their battle cries have been turned into mega-tough anagrams. Can you unscramble them?

1 "On Roll On Doggy!"
Hint: It's a Tech Skylander

2 "Lighted Thine Grin!"
Hint: It's a Water Skylander

NO **CHAIN** NO **GAIN!**

SILENT BUT **DEADLY!**

3 **"No Brunt Orb!"**
Hint: It's a Fire Skylander

4 **"Little Used Bandy!"**
Hint: It's a Life Skylander

5 **"An Aching Onion!"**
Hint: It's an Undead Skylander

BORN TO BURN!

RIDE THE LIGHTNING!

NO GOLD NO GLORY!

BRING THE BOOM!   FEAR THE FISH!   IT'S FEEDING TIME!

6 **"I'm Niftiest Edge!"**
Hint: It's an Earth Skylander

7 **"A Half Mad Recluse!"**
Hint: It's an Air Skylander

8 **"Hot Ribbon Gem!"**
Hint: It's another Tech Skylander

9 **"Exquisite Sonar Flatters!"**
Hint: It's a Magic Skylander

10 **"If Fresh Hate!"**
Hint: It's another Water Skylander

MY SCORE

/10

ANSWERS

1 "No Gold No Glory!"
2 "Ride the Lightning!"
3 "Born to Burn!"
4 "Silent but Deadly!"
5 "No Chain No Gain!"
6 "It's Feeding Time!"
7 "Full Scream Ahead!"
8 "Bring the Boom!"
9 "Axe First Questions Later!"
10 "Fear the Fish!"

WORD WARRIORS

Word Count

How many times do the individual Elements appear in this grid?

Magic =

Tech =

Earth =

Air =

Fire =

Water =

Life =

Undead =

MY SCORE

/8

170

```
U D F T Y H V M U N D E A D F
N Y O C T S N A A D V H A C I
D C L R A E E G R C O C N N R
E E A E F O L I T H C E Y I E
A E L I Z A B C E A R T H E T
D H L M R A Y P C A I T R I C
F I R E K J R O H J E R N D E
W E T S E F I L T C F L I K F
G A A R D Y A P A L I F E N I
W T R I A H O N D S L K Y L L
A B N D C I G A M H C E T E R
S D A E D N U S P T Y R O E H
E X T G L U M D S R H A R R N
K D S M A S D T E A R E O I N
E F I L C A U N D E A D V F A
```

171

Code Breaker

Can you break Stealth Elf's code to reveal a message from the Skylands story scrolls?

A	B	C	D	E	F	G	H	I	J	K	L	M
17		13								23	5	7

N	O	P	Q	R	S	T	U	V	W	X	Y	Z
				18	22							

MY
SCORE
/22

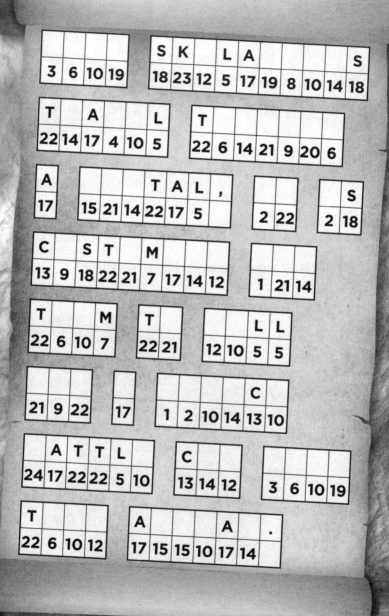

3	6	10	19

S	K		L	A					S
18	23	12	5	17	19	8	10	14	18

T		A			L
22	14	17	4	10	5

T						
22	6	14	21	9	20	6

A
17

		T	A	L	,
15	21	14	22	17	5

2	22

	S
2	18

C		S	T		M			
13	9	18	22	21	7	17	14	12

1	21	14

T			M
22	6	10	7

T	
22	21

		L	L
12	10	5	5

21	9	22

17

				C	
1	2	10	14	13	10

	A	T	T	L	
24	17	22	22	5	10

C		
13	14	12

3	6	10	19

T			
22	6	10	12

A				A		.
17	15	15	10	17	14	

WHICH SKYLANDER ARE YOU?

Your quest is almost over, so why not take a break to find out which Skylander you are most like?

1 **Which is your favourite element?**

- **A** Magic
- **B** Water
- **C** Tech
- **D** Fire
- **E** Life
- **F** Undead
- **G** Air
- **H** Earth

2 What kind of food do you prefer?

A A bit of everything
B Seafood
C Mexican
D Anything hot and spicy
E Vegetables
F Ghosts
G Meat and lots of it
H Rock cakes

3 What kind of party would you most like to be invited to?

A I don't care as long as my friends are there
B A pool party
C Paintball
D A beach party
E A hide and seek championship
F I don't care as long as there's loads to eat
G One with lots of games
H I don't like parties. Too many people

4 Which of the following best describes your personality?

A Fearless
B Loyal
C Manic
D Hot-headed
E Sneaky
F Creepy
G Heroic
H Solitary

5 Which of these skills would you most like to learn?

A How to fly
B Fishing
C Shooting
D Keeping my temper in check
E Tracking
F Cooking
G Learn skills? I'm pretty perfect already!
H Rock climbing

6 Where do you like to go on holiday?

A Anywhere as long as we fly there
B By the sea
C The Wild West
D Anywhere hot
E A nice green place
F Somewhere where there isn't much sun
G Somewhere sunny so I can show off my muscles
H Somewhere where there are no crowds

7 What kind of films do you like?

A Superhero films

B Romance

C Westerns

D Action movies

E Spy movies

F Scary films

G Sports films

H Silent movies. I don't like noise

8 What are you like when working in a team?

A I'm a natural leader

B I look after my teammates

C I'm eager to hit the target

D I'm fine unless people annoy me

E I keep quiet and get the job done

F People are sometimes a little scared of me

G I'm happy to help. After all, I'm good – really good

H I'd rather work alone, but I'll play my part

You are like:

Mostly As: Spyro
You're courageous and strong-willed; a natural leader and a born hero.

Mostly Bs: Gill Grunt
You have a big heart and are always ready to protect your friends.

Mostly Cs: Trigger Happy
You're fast, furious and quick to jump into action. You're one wild guy!

Mostly Ds: Eruptor
You need to keep your temper in check, but are brave and fearless.

Mostly Es: Stealth Elf
Quick and dependable, everyone wants you on their team.

Mostly Fs: Ghost Roaster
You have a dark side, but you fight for what's right. Oh, and you like your food!

Mostly Gs: Lightning Rod
You're always the best at what you do – and you know it.

Mostly Hs: Prism Break
You like your own company, but you can always be relied on.

MASTER EON'S MEGA QUIZ

Congratulations young Portal Master. You have almost completed your quest. But the last challenge will stretch your knowledge to the limit. How many of these fiendishly difficult questions can you answer correctly?

1 **What happens to Skylanders when they are defeated in battle?**
   A They turn evil
   B They portal back home to Eon's citadel to recover
   C They turn into statues

2 **How old was Eon when he first activated a Portal?**
   A 6   **B** 7   **C** 8

3 **What was the name of the greatest catapult ever built?**
 A The Leveler   **B** The Flinger   **C** The Lobber

4 **Before he was a Skylander, what was Boomer a member of?**
 A The Troll Army
 B The Sheep Grenadiers
 C The Cyclops Navy

5 **Why did the Molekin all go bald?**
 A They smelled one of Kaos' socks
 B They tried to use crude oil as hair tonic
 C An evil wizard stole their hair for use in a potion

6 **What is the name of the red dragon knight who protects the Dragon's Peak?**
A Flame
B Flavius
C Sparx

7 **Which of his own minions does Kaos really hate?**
A The Evil Ent
B The Evil Ninja
C The Evil Witch

8 **What can Skylanders gain from a visit to Persephone?**
A Minty fresh breath
B Upgraded abilities
C Moustaches

9 **How many legs does a Gargantula have?**
A Four   **B** Six   **C** Eight

10 Who is the oldest of the Mabu group known as the Mystic Seekers?

A Humfry **B** Beaufort **C** Fargus

11 Who is the son of the oldest member of the Mystic Seekers?

A Tizwig **B** Wendel **C** Esmerelle

12 What is the name of the baker who persuaded the Undead to eat pies rather than people?

A Batterboy
B Batterson
C Battersby

13 **What is the name of the small, green creatures that live inside Skylands keyholes?**
A Lockwizard imps
B Lockbuddy imps
C Lockmaster imps

14 **What kind of trolls pilot Gun Snouts?**
A Troll greasemonkeys
B Trollverines
C Troll grenadier

15 **What can Water spell punks summon?**
A Giant Undead fish
B Giant chattering clams
C Giant drops of freezing water

16 What was the name of the First Lord of the Undead?
A Malefor
B Mortalannis
C Murkyana

17 How many horns do cyclops mammoths have?
A 1 **B** 2 **C** 3

18 Which creatures invented balloons?
A The Drow **B** The Mabu **C** Chompies

19 Which creature did Kaos summon to destroy the Core of Light?

A The Wyvern

B The Hydra

C The Basilisk

20 How do you turn Rhu-Barbs back into Rhu-Babies?

A Stamp on them

B Make them eat broccoli

C Defeat the spell punk who grew them in the first place

21 What appears on Goliath Drow's shields when they charge?

A Spikes B Kaos' face C Stars

22 **How long did the Arkeyan Weapon Master sleep?**
- **A** 1,000 years
- **B** 10,000 years
- **C** 100,000 years

23 **What is the name of Dragon King Ramses' evil brother?**
- **A** Vartek
- **B** Vortex
- **C** Vathek

24 **What does Clam-Tron 4000 turn into bombs?**
- **A** Clams
- **B** Pearls
- **C** Apples

25 **What shape is the medal on General Robot's chest?**
   A A circle
   B A triangle
   C A cross

26 **How much money does Terrafin claim to be owed by Kaos?**
   A Three guineas
   B Five dollars
   C Ten euros

27 **What component of the Core of Light helps water flow from the Eternal Water Source?**
   A Twin Spout of Aqua-Exclusa
   B Twin Spouts of Atlantic-Pacific-Caspian
   C Twin Spouts of Ocea-Major-Minor

28 What is the name of Skylands' banker?
A Cashley **B** Richman **C** Auric

29 What are the icy cousins of the flame imps called?
A Frozen fiends
B Ice pops
C Chilly candles

30 Eon discovered he was a Portal Master by accident, after transporting his mentor where?
A The Desert of Columns
B The Forest of Fear
C The Dirt Seas

MY
SCORE
/30

FINAL SCORE

Time to add up those scores, young Portal Master. Write your grand total here and see how well you did.

MY TOTAL

0-25: Not that powerful ... yet!
Hmmm. I'm not sure you've been paying attention. I'll get Hugo to dig out some Skylands history books for you. Don't worry – we all had to start somewhere.

26 - 150: Showing Portal Promise!
You're on the road to becoming a legendary Portal Master. Keep practising and you'll soon be named among the greats, like, er, me.

151 - 300: One To Watch!
Well done, that's a good effort. Get to know your Skylanders a bit better and you'll soon be a real force to reckon with.

301 - 499: Super Skylands Skills!
Impressive. You're almost as knowledgeable as me – although I think my beard is better. Either way, Kaos had better watch out.

500+: Portal Master Supreme!
Congratulations – what an amazing score!
Skylands is in safe hands. Darkness will
never fall while you are a Portal Master.

Master Eon